The Genealogist and the Project Manager:

A "How To" for the New Genealogist and Historian

Daniel G. Anderson, PMP

ISBN-10: 1484132033
ISBN-13: 978-1484132036

DEDICATION

To the Love of my life, my instructor in genealogy, and my best friend –
Margie.

CONTENTS

ACKNOWLEDGMENTS, PREFACE AND EDITION NOTES

My wife Margie is the Genealogist of our family, and I'm a rank amateur! I am also more of the historian in the family. But I'm also a certified Project Management Professional (PMP) by the Project Management Institute (PMI). That's like a CPA in the finance world.

I enjoy working with Margie and dabbling in my own genealogy questions (such as "Who was the Caton Progenitor in the United States?"), but I have some basic questions about genealogy and history. Since genealogy is disciplined study (an '-logy' is "a combining form used in the names of sciences or bodies of knowledge: paleontology; theology.") there must be a standard process and set of tools to support this study. And there is!!!!!

I find there is a strong connection between Genealogy and History. To me Genealogy is the study of how people and families are linked while History at its very base is the study of how those people lived and what they accomplished. I find that there are processes and tools to support this study!!!

And the two sets of processes are VERY compatible!!!! If there is a standard process and set of tools, there must be projects and programs!

And if there are projects and programs I can keep track of where I'm going, where I am, where I was – and KEEP ORGANIZED!

And you ask "So what?" If I have a set of tools to conduct my family history study (genealogy) in an organized, professional manner I can get more accomplished – AND ENJOY IT MORE! I can be more productive and less frustrated. For example I can plan where and when I do my research. So, I hope to share this joy – and knowledge – with you!

These ideas do not REPLACE your genealogy, research and history tools – they are a method to organize your efforts as you USE the tools.

NOTES for the Second Edition:

Examples used throughout this book are from my own research.

I have expanded my discussion of history as it relates to genealogy and the processes presented in this book because my two professional passions, history and project management, have come to influence each other.

I hope this book fuels and aides in your own study of Family History and Genealogy!

Daniel G. Anderson, PMP
March, 2012

NOTES for this Third Edition:

For the past year I have been leading focus groups learning about genealogy and writing family histories. As often happens, the facilitator learns as much as the group! Based on this I have added details about copy right, sources and their repositories, publication information, etc. that we have developed in these sessions.

I wish to thank the leadership, staff, members and participants at the Midwest Historical and Genealogical Society in Wichita, Kansas for their help, expertise and questions.

I am now the Executive Director of the Midwest Historic Masonic Lodge Association, Inc. in Wichita, Kansas. This has lead me to talking with Masons researching and writing community histories. I have included additional insights gained from these invaluable discussions.

Daniel G. Anderson, PMP
April 2013

PROJECT MANAGEMENT, GENEALOGY AND HISTORY

What is Genealogy?

One source is generally consistent with what I've read. Wikipedia defines "Genealogy (from Greek: γενεα, genea, "family"; and λόγος, logos, "knowledge") is the study and tracing of families. Modern genealogical research is a complex process that involves more than affixing a collection of names to a pedigree chart. Rather, genealogy involves identifying ancestral or descendant families by using historical records to establish biological, genetic, or familial kinship. Reliable conclusions are based on the quality of sources (ideally original records, rather than derivatives), the information within those sources (ideally primary or firsthand information, rather than secondary or secondhand information), and the evidence that can be drawn (directly or indirectly) from that information. In many instances, genealogists must skillfully assemble indirect or circumstantial evidence to build a case for identity and kinship. All evidence and conclusions, together with the documentation that supports them, is then assembled to create a cohesive "genealogy" or "family history." Traditionalists may differentiate between these last two terms, using the former to describe skeletal accounts of kinship (aka family trees) and the latter as a "fleshing out" of lives and personal histories. However, historical, social, and family context is in any case essential to achieving correct identification of individuals and relationships."

So Genealogy is more than researching and recording names, birth dates, death dates, etc.! Genealogy includes the study of the family history, the grass-roots of regional and national history! As such information must be meticulously and consistently sourced and analyzed.

And knowledge horded is wasted. Therefore the results of our genealogy studies must be shared in some form. However care must be taken so improper or incomplete information is not published in the wrong environment. Disseminate your knowledge – but be careful of the audience and be respectful of copyright information.

What is History and the Connection to Genealogy?

History, to me, answers these questions: "Who?"; "did What?"; "When?"; "Where?"; "Why?", and "What does it mean to us today?". History teaches by using examples from the past to build our foundations to effectively create and guide our decisions for the future.

Genealogy gives us the basic facts of "Who?", (maybe) "did What?", "When?", and "Where?". It is up to us as historians to connect these bits of facts to deduce both the "Why?" and "What does it mean to us today?".

The connection between history and genealogy are even tighter in the niches of Community and Family History. These subjects are, for many, the most intriguing an important. They answer the questions "How did this family (or group) relate to their social and cultural environment?" and "How did the environment affect them?". For example, when I research a neighborhood or a social group in a community I complete (to the extent possible identified in my project plan) a genealogy study of each individual and family involved. Also, when I work on a genealogy I study the history of the community they are involved in and how it affected them. This leads to understanding where to look for the next genealogic discovery and the clarification of an new historical fact.

What is a Project and Project Management?

PMI defines a project as "… a temporary endeavor undertaken to create a unique product, service, or result." "Temporary means that every project has a definite beginning and a definite end." Project Management is the discipline of managing the solution of a project using the processes and tools of the supported discipline – in this case, Genealogy and History. The Project Management concepts include the scalable processes of Integration, Scope, Time, Cost, Quality, Human Resources, Communications, Risk and Procurement Management.

What does Project Management Have to do with Them?

Project Management is the discipline of defining, planning, executing and finalizing a specific measurable task-oriented finite goal. If the goal is to research and document a genealogic or historic subject (individual, family, family line or community), Project Management provides the tools to define, track, manage, report and reach that goal. It helps define the goal in workable, defined and measurable concepts so we know what the goal is, when we've reached the goal (or how close we are to it), the resources (money, people, books, subscriptions, repositories, associations, etc.) needed and time required. The goal is defined in the SCOPE of the project, and relates directly to the TIME and RESOURCES – the three-legged-stool of Project Management.

This concept is critical if you are going to hire a professional genealogist or historian! How else are you going to estimate and gage the professional's success in reaching the study goal in the allotted (and charged!) time!

And since your own time is precious – how do you estimate and gage your time and resources?!?

Simple Project Management techniques help you keep on track and (since we all have interruptions!) pick up where you left off.

A Note on Simple Flow Charts

The diagrams in this book use basic standard flow chart symbols. For those not familiar with these symbols, here is the definitions.

Terminator – the start or end of the process.

Process – a task or tasks that needs to be done.

Decision Point – the point that requires the answer to a question.

Document – a physical document recording the results.

Defined Process – a series of related tasks that is defined either in documentation or in another process flow chart.

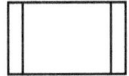

Arrows indicate the next step to be completed, they define the logic flow. If there is a label ('Yes' or 'No'), that arrow is the one to follow based on the answer to the Decision Point question.

When there is a connection between two diagrams (usually if the diagram is too big for one page) there is a 'Connector' symbol in each diagram. The connection symbols have matching letters, so when you 'leave' one diagram at connector 'A' you 'enter' the other diagram at connector 'A'.

A

GENERAL RESEARCH PROCESS

When I studied for my post graduate degree, one of the first books required to be studied was "Practical Research Planning and Design", Fifth Edition by Paul D Leedy.   Key elements for our study start in Chapter 1: The Dimensions of Research, Dimension Three: What is Research?. Leedy lays out eight distinct characteristics:

- "Research begins in the mind of the researcher."

- "Research demands that the researcher articulate a specific goal for the investigative process. ... the statement of the problem for research."

- "Research demands a specific plan of procedure. ... the research plan."

- "Research generally recognizes that a frontal attack on the entire problem is too much to attempt at one time. Every problem can be divided into subproblems."

- "Research is generally guided by constructs called hypotheses."

- "Research accepts certain critical assumptions ..."

- "Research countenances only specific, measurable data ..."

- "Research is, by nature, a circular or more exactly, as helical process."

These characteristics lead Leedy to two key processes: The Research Cycle and the Helical Concept of the Research Process.   The Research Cycle lays out the steps to research and answer a specific research problem (characteristics 2 and3) while the Helical Concept relates to concepts 4 and

8 to the fact that the answers to one question lead to the questions of the next problem! Now we can research one problem statement (project or subproject) and relate it to a larger problem statement (project or program). We will discuss projects, subprojects and programs later.

Steps of the General Research Cycle

Leedy lays out 6 steps in the Research Cycle. These steps are:

- "Research begins with a problem: an unanswered question in the mind of the researcher."

- "Research sees the goal in a clear statement of the problem."

- "Research subdivides the problem into appropriate subproblems. Each subproblem seeks guidance through an appropriate hypothesis." Here Leedy adds a note: "Research holds the hypotheses until all the facts are in and interpreted. At that point the hypotheses are supported or rejected." These hypotheses are created in Step 3, used in Step 4 and answered in Step 6.

- "Research posits tentative solutions to the problem(s) through appropriate hypotheses. These hypotheses direct the researcher to the facts."

- "Research looks for facts directed by the hypotheses and guided by the problem. The facts are collected and organized."

- "Research interprets the meaning of the facts which leads to a resolution of the problem, thus confirming or rejecting the hypotheses and providing an answer to the question which began the research cycle."

Leedy's Helical Concept

The Helical Concept of the Research Process takes this one giant step forward! Here Leedy provides seven steps which are:

- "A questioning mind becomes aware of a research problem."

- "The research problem is fractionated into logical subparts called subproblems."

- "Preliminary facts – data – are assembled"

- "and these lead to statements of tentative research hypotheses."

- "The quest for more facts – additional data – continues."

- "The accumulation of additional data and their analysis and interpretation leads to the discovery of their meaning."

- "The analysis of the data suddenly becomes a discovery, resulting in a resolution of a subproblem, or perhaps, the main research problem."

And here he adds the key connector! "The resolution of one problem situation always reveals additional and related problems that need resolution. And so, the process of research spirals onward in a continuous quest after he discovery of new knowledge." In other words, if we have resolved a subproblem we move to the next subproblem with a new Step 1. If we have answered the main research problem we have completed the research cycle and move on.

"All very nice – and very academic!" you say? I agree! So we need to put more 'meat' (tools and definitions) on these 'bones'!

COMMON GENEALOGY AND HISTORY RESEARCH PROCESSES

I have found four Genealogy Research Processes, and have issues with each. There is the Drake Process which is the least controlled and the most flexible. Next it the BYU process that is a good general start, but for our purposes is far too vague. Then there is a process published on the internet by Karen Clifford, AG which I find very useful in many instances. Finally, Kimberly Powell's process published on the internet is also very useful in many circumstances.

These four research processes provide us with very useful tools – but not quite enough for managing a genealogy or history project! The first step is to understand these valuable tools. Then we will see how to use these tools in a true genealogy or history project.

"Start Writing" Process

Paul Drake, in his book "In Search of Family History: A Starting Place" recommends to start writing and finish when you are done. This is the easiest process to use but is also the least rigorous. It is very useful if you are an expert and you are writing a short article. The process depends the least on evidence. And how do you know when you are 'done'? How much time and effort should you devote to this effort? How do you support your argument/hypothesis? There are places to use this process, but is also the process I use the least.

<u>BYU Genealogy Research Process</u>

A general definition of genealogy identifies a process – identifying an individual, identify the family relationships, and researching – is often cited as the "never-ending genealogy process". A more concise definition from the BYU Broadcasting DVD "Ancestors: The Research Process" provides these steps:

"Write Down What You Know"

"Decide What You Want To Learn"

"Choose a Source of Information"

"Learn From The Source"

"Use What You Learn"

This process in repeated by going from Step 5 to Step 1. The BYU Genealogy Research Process seems to further define the General Research Process defined by Leedy! It provides the next step from the 'academic' to the 'usable' process.

But a 'usable' process must have a place to start and a place to exit! And it must produce something, it must be reproducible, and it must be testable. The BYU process is a good starting place to develop a usable process, but it is not a usable tool for a Project Manager by itself. There is a define place for this tool, which we will look at in the Anderson Genealogy Process.

Clifford Genealogy Research Process

Karen Clifford, AG, in her book Genealogy, the Internet, and Your Genealogy Computer Program, published by the Genealogical Publishing Company, from an excerpt available on Genealogy.com at http://www.genealogy.com/84_clifford_print.html (30 July 3011), identifies 8 steps in a circular flow. The Clifford Research Cycle is:

1. Set a goal

2. Decide which source to use

3. Locate that source

4. Search that source

5. Copy the information

6. Evaluate the information

7. Use the results, and

8. Organize and reorganize.

This is much better for a process – it has a starting point (”1.”), it produces something (“7.”), and it is reproducible and testable (“8.”)!

I have one small, but significant, addition to the Clifford Process to make it usable for a project. A step 9 needs to be added – Evaluate if the Goal identified in Step 1 is met. If the goal is met then this instance of the process ends, if the goal is not met then the process is continued. The result is the Modified Clifford Research Process. See Figure 1. It is most useful if you don't know much about your subject. Once a useful amount of information is developed, you could transition to the Modified Powell Genealogy Research Process.

And one caution – Step 5 states "Copy the information". Ensure you are not plagiarizing, record the Source Information. See the discussion on Source Record.

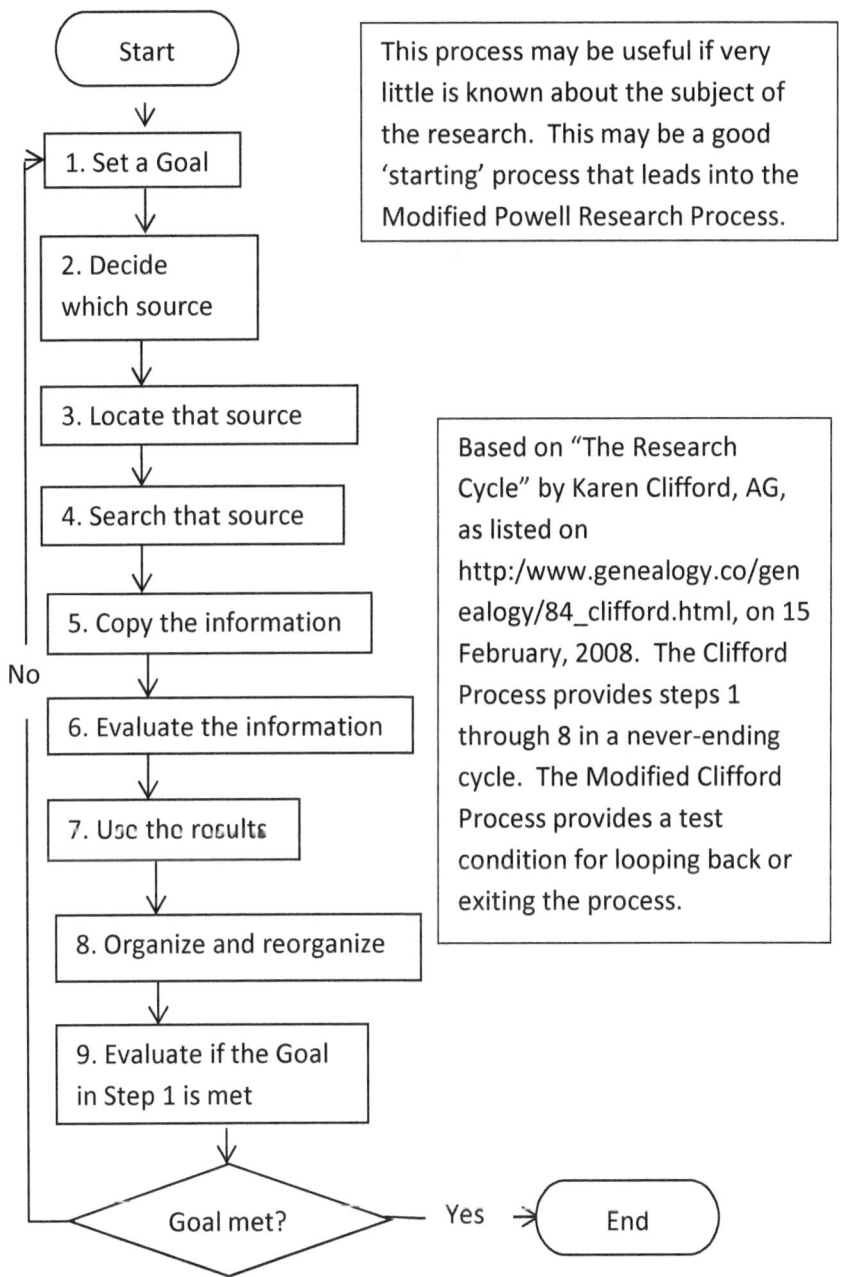

This process may be useful if very little is known about the subject of the research. This may be a good 'starting' process that leads into the Modified Powell Research Process.

Based on "The Research Cycle" by Karen Clifford, AG, as listed on http:/www.genealogy.co/genealogy/84_clifford.html, on 15 February, 2008. The Clifford Process provides steps 1 through 8 in a never-ending cycle. The Modified Clifford Process provides a test condition for looping back or exiting the process.

Figure 1 - Modified Clifford Research Process

Powell Genealogy Research Process

Kimberly Powell provides a 10-step process . By adding a qualifier to Step 5 and a decision point after step 10 we have a process that also meets our requirements! These steps are:

1. Select an individual or family to research,

2. Identify what you already know

3. Bone up on background info

4. Survey existing information

5. Set (or review) a goal

6. Decide which type of record is most likely to contain the information

7. Locate and search the record

8. Copy the pertinent info

9. Analyze and evaluate the new information, and

10. Document/record the results.

The Modified Powell Genealogy Research Process is very useful if you know some information and you are seeking to corroborate information or expand on previously identified information. See Figure 2.

Again a caution – Step 8 states "Copy the pertinent info". Ensure you are not plagiarizing when you record the Source Information. See the discussion on Source Record in the Anderson Process Chapter.

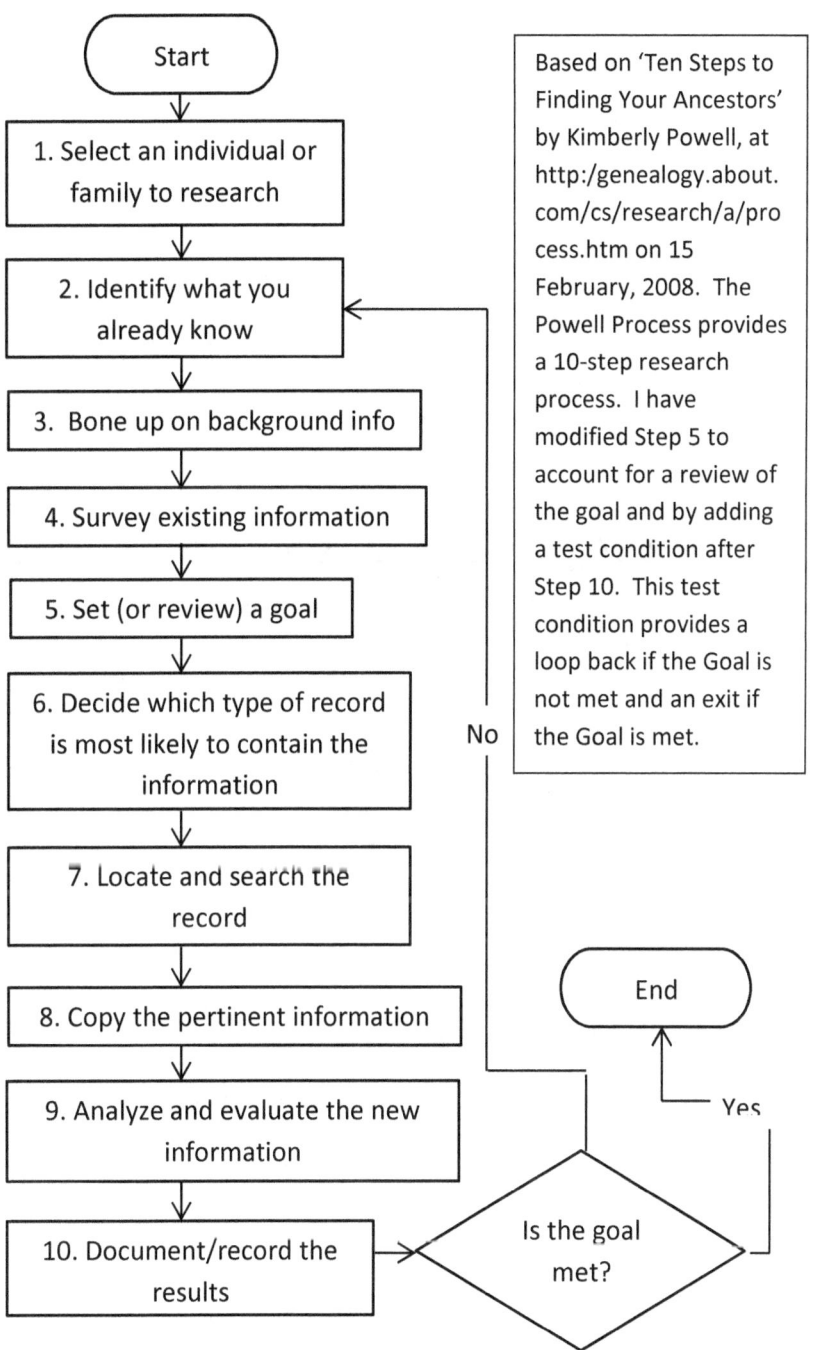

Figure 2 – Modified Powell Genealogy Research Process

ANDERSON GENEALOGY AND HISTORY PROCESS

Why the Anderson Genealogy and History Process?

When I first asked "How do I conduct genealogical and historical research?" I was told "Identify what you know, record what you known, identify what you don't know, form long-term and short-term goals to research what you don't know." Hmm, sounds good but you will never exit the research!!!!!! There must be a cycle! If your research answers your goal then record your research and move out of the research process. If it does NOT answer the goal then record your research, refine you goal with the new information and the research again.

And what happens if you learned something that relates to another project, person or family? If you don't record and file your information that research will be lost!

And there is MUCH more to Genealogy and History than just researching and recording. Information without analysis is just "dead information", but if you analyze that information you have "live history"! As I mentioned earlier – knowledge that is not shared is useless! So let's expand on the Research Processes and Genealogy Research Processes – and use them in the broader Anderson Genealogy and History Process context.

When the scope is defined, we have DEFINED the research goals for ONE PROBLEM STATEMENT. This answers the first two steps of the BYU Research Process with "Identify and Record what is Known" followed by "Identify what is not known - write as Research Process Goals". With this accomplished, we can now choose which of our Genealogy and History Research Processes to use as tools. And when our

Genealogy and History Research Process is done, we move into recording followed by analysis. Finally, when our scope conditions are met we can finish with synthesis and publication. Thus, with an expanded Anderson Genealogy and History Process, we can define our results, manage the process, include repeatability and testability, resulting in a finished product. The resulting process flow is in Figure 3.

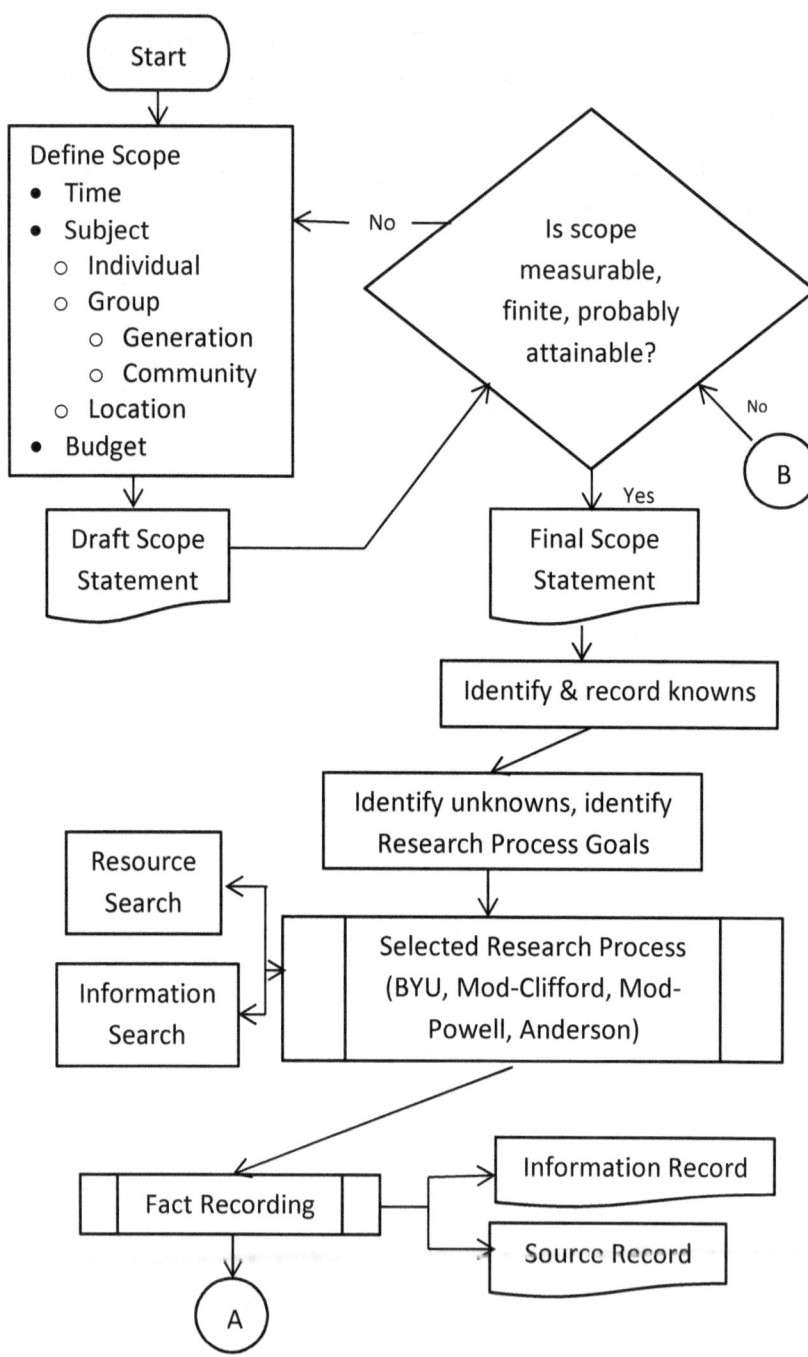

Figure 3 – Anderson Genealogy and History Process

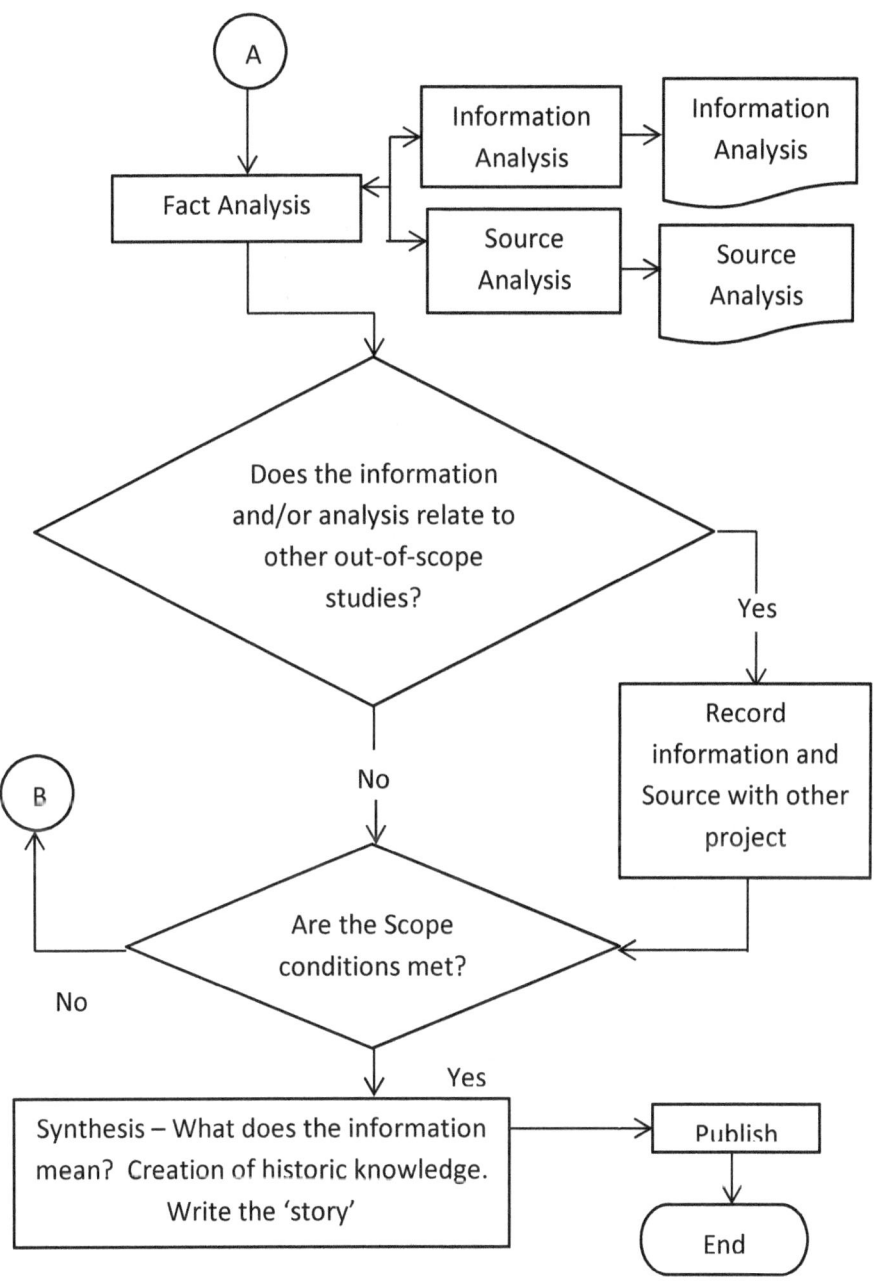

Figure 3 – Anderson Genealogy and History Process (Continued)

<u>Define Scope, Programs, Projects and Subprojects</u>

As we saw in "The Research Process" we can break down our large genealogy or history problem (research the Caton family) into manageable 'chunks' in our problem statement. These manageable 'chunks' have defined limits of subject (problem) and resources (time, repositories, locations, trips, money and people). Now we have something we can measure – how long will it take, how much will it cost, and how close to an answer are we! This problem statement is known in Project Management as the Scope Statement. And since the whole Caton family obviously a large effort or program, we can break it down into subprojects. This is where we can use the BYU Genealogy Research Process, especially steps 1 through 3, to great advantage!

<u>Scope</u>

Let's start by defining the scope of our study. We need to define what we will study and what resources we will need. The study can be an individual, a family (parents and children), a family group (several specified generations) or a community (Salem, MA in 1635 for example). Then we can define how much time we are going to spend (either by calendar reference or by event reference), what resources we will likely need, followed by how much money to spend.

The scope statement takes into account the time required (say the next two weeks), subject (John Caton's arrival in Virginia for example) and budget (additional books, subscriptions, memberships or trips to Virginia for example). The statement should be written – otherwise in two weeks you may forget what your budget is!

Now answer the question "Is my statement measurable, finite and probably attainable?" This is the first diamond in the diagram. If the answer is 'no' we need to further refine our Scope Statement – BUT DON'T GET RID OF THE DRAFTS! We can use these to identify Scope Statements for Programs and other Projects and Subprojects. If the answer is 'yes' then we can move on to executing our project (after we have defined all the Scope Statements!).

Here is also where we subdivide the question into subquestions – programs, projects and subprojects.

Now we know when we will be 'done' with each effort! And we can identify when we have ventured too far and are working on something else – but not on the project we defined!

Programs

PMI defines a program as "A group of related projects managed in a coordinated way to obtain benefits and control not available from managing them individually. Programs may include elements of related work outside the scope of the discrete projects in the program." In other words, a genealogic program would be large and less defined than a project and would include many projects. It may also include discussions on a family web site or in a genealogic society.

An example program would be "Write a book on the history of the Caton family in North America". It will include projects on each member of the Caton family, on Caton family groups and membership in the Caton Family Web Site. One of your initial Scope Statements will probably answer this requirement, but will not be defined enough to be a Project Scope Statement.

A detailed discussion of programs is out of the scope of this book, but this should give you enough to intuitively start working on your genealogic program.

Projects

A project is "A temporary endeavor undertaken to create a unique product, service, or result." By temporary we mean one defined time that will only be done once because the results are unique. For example, my study of the "John Caton family in Virginia from 1680 to the early 1700's for the Caton Family Book Program to be completed in the next two months" would be a project. I will only study that family group one time for this particular program. I may return to the study of this family group at another time, but it will be for another program.

If there is no program, the Project Scope Statement may be "Identify, record and publish to the Caton Family Web Site the possible connection of John Caton who emigrated to the Colony of Virginia in 1681 to the known and published Caton family tree information". This is a project definition with an event-driven time frame – the answer to the proposed connection is proven or disproved.

Subprojects

"Subproject. A smaller portion of the overall project created when a project is subdivided into more manageable components or pieces. ..." Subprojects are developed and managed like projects. They form the helical of Leedy's Helical Concept. Therefore, two subprojects may be "Research and record the land records of John Caton who emigrated in 1681 using the Virginia Archives and other land record offices" and "Research and record the marriage and children of John Caton who emigrated to Virginia in 1681 in the official vital statistics and wills recorded in the Virginia Archives."

Now I have a Genealogical Program with one Genealogical Project and two Genealogical Subprojects that are detailed enough for measurement. Since the two subprojects relate to the project, they have the same time boundaries. And the questions are either answered or not answered.

Identify and Record what is Known

This is the same point made in the Leedy, BYU, Clifford and Powell processes. Start from known (but NOT assumed or unsupported) information. Record known information about the people, places, times and locations you are studying. Also record the known sources – you will need this to find more sources and to keep from "retreading old ground".

Then record assumptions and unsupported ('facts' without a source identified) data. Do not mix these with the facts! This action will help you with the next step. Assumptions are 'guesses' that need researched and until they are supported and sourced cannot be relied upon for analysis. As such, they are NOT 'Known'.

Use your familiar recording tools – family group sheets, individual record sheets, etc. And a 'trade secret' – keep organized! When you get interrupted for a few days you can return to where you left off without starting over!

Record Research Process Goals

Expand the statements about what is not known – write them as Research Process Goals.

Here is Leedy's Helical Concept Step 3! Further define the Project Scope Statement to specify what is not known – and therefore what you are looking for. If you do not know what you are looking for, how will you know when you have found it?

Record this information, along with your assumptions and unsupported data in your research project notes. This information will keep your search on course and productive.

As you research, you can turn the unsupported data into useful information as you add the sources. This data becomes known information and will be recorded with the source information in the Genealogy Analysis Step.

As you research you will prove or disprove assumptions. In the Genealogy Analysis Step you will record these also. Record the proven assumptions as known information. Record the disproven assumptions so you (and others) will not fall into their traps in the future!

Select Research Process

Now we get to the heart of the process – the fun part! Use the processes we covered to conduct the research. The art of project management involves selecting the correct tool. I would use the "Start Writing" or the BYU Process when only family or very limited informaton is availabe. Then I would use the Modified Clifford Process for those projects where some research has uncovered repositories, archives and resources but only a few are known. Since you can move between the process tools that seem to work the best, you may want to start with the "Start Writing" Process. When you learn a bit more (subjective, I know!), after checking the scope statement you can move to the BYU Process. Next, as the scope matures or the information becomes more detailed you can change to the Modified Clifford Process and finally transition to the Modified Powel Process.

NOTE: THE SEARCH AND RECORDING PROCESSES ARE COMPLETED INTERACTIVELY - AT THE SAME TIME. RECORD WHAT YOU FIND WHEN YOU FIND IT! OFTEN THE INFORMATION AND SOURCE ANALYSIS , AS WELL AS THE ANALYSIS RECORDING, ARE COMPLETED AT THIS TIME – HOWEVER THIS SHOULD BE AN INITIAL ANALYSIS AND RECORDING ONLY. FINAL ANALYSIS AND RECORDING MUST INCLUDE INFORMATION GAINED OVER THE ENTIRE LIFE OF THE PROJECT.

Information Search

You can start searching for information in those sources you identified earlier. You have those sources that gave you "What I Know" information. Check these same sources for additional information and leads to other sources and repositories. Continue developing the information by moving from source to source. Check out the bibliographies, research help and internet.

Remember to record what you find, as well as what you do not find. If you expected to find some information in a source and the information is not there, that may mean something. For example, George is listed in the 1905 State Census and 1910 Federal Census living in Georgetown. You look in the 1915 State Census and he is not listed. The fact that George is not found in 1915 needs recorded so you can start looking for him! He may not have been home, his name may be misspelled, he may have moved, or he may have died – but further research is required to find him!

Keep in mind that in your research you may (and very probably will) find information about people, places, sources and repositories not related to this project, but do relate to other projects in your program, other projects or other subprojects. Record the information and sources, and bring them through the process with this cycle – otherwise you will have to duplicate your efforts later or, even worse, you will forget the information and it will be lost! We will account for this information at the end of the process.

When you are using transcriptions ensure you report transcription errors to the repository and/or the transcriber. Remember that transcribers can make well meaning but critical errors. By providing your corrections you can help the historical community. Provide your analysis of the error which may lead to other researchers finding what they are looking for! When using transcriptions refer to the original document if at all possible.

Often there is additional information in the original that is not reflected in the index or transcription. For example you may find an individual's occupation, street address, and other related individuals in the area when looking at an original census document – information that is not often captured in the transcription.

Record you information and record where you got the information. The information is called a citation. Where you got the information is called a source. A repository is where the source is stored. See further details in the Informatin (Citation) Record and the Source Record sections.

Source Search

Try searching by source titles such as family histories and known repositories such as the Virginia Archives and census information. Remember to always record the sources in the next step, you may want to use them again – or you may never want to use them again – based on your source analysis. The future use of sources depends on the results of the Genealogical Analysis step. Keep in mind that there are now many fictitious family tree files now on the internet!

The Source and Repository information in your initial Sources will lead you to more information! Check the bibliographies of the sources you already have. Search the internet, the library – your Initial Repository – for more sources.

Identifying and Recording Repositories

Ideally you will visit each repository one time. In reality you may visit each repository several times as you gain an understanding of your subject and sources. Your initial sources identify your initial repositories. From both the initial source and repository you can start to develop a list of potential repositories to search. Staff in some repositories can lead you to other repositories that are not obvious, so don't be shy about asking the librarians questions!

Sources and repositories lead to other sources and repositories. Here is a list of types of repositories and sources to help you in brainstorming and finding more sources:

- Family and friends

- Local Historical Society

- Local Genealogical Society

- Libraries

- Archives (Government, university, college and private)

- Maps and property records

- Newspapers and periodicals

- Journals and diaries

- Government Offices

  - County Court Houses

  - City Hall

  - State Capital

  - National Archives and Offices

- o Police records

- Museums

- Universities

- Churches

- Funeral Homes

- Cemeteries

- Community Organizations (Masons, Odd Fellows, etc.)

Genealogical and Historical Recording

Use your normal recording tools such as Family Sheets and Indiviual Sheets used in genealogy. There are many publications regarding how to use these well established genealogical recording tools, so I will not discuss them in this book.

Information (Citation) Record

Record what you found, and what you did not find, in your information search. These records are the facts that, when analyzed, become the answers to your Scope Statement. They are the results you are looking for on your collection quest. This information will be the basis of the Analysis step.

This step is where researchers get into trouble with plagurism! Proper ethical recording of citations is critical to good supportable professional historical writing.

A Citation is a statement of what you found in the source. This includes a fact you record based on what you read or saw, a paraphrase of the information, or a quotation. The original idea you record based on reading a source document is your intelectual property, but it must be connected to the source you are using to support that idea. A paraphrase or a quotation are NOT your original idea and must be referred to the source.

Under Copyright Law (see additional discussion in the Publishing section), researchers may freely copy a limited amout of information (rule of thumb – a paragraph but no more than three pages). This information must be identified as a paraphrase or quotation, and the source must be recorded and credited in the documtent (foot- or end-notes). If more information OR an image is used there must be a release, license or agreement between you and the author/creator.

Copyright laws protect you and other researchers and authors. Original information that you capture by writing or recording it are protected as your intelectual property at that time. For a full discussion of Copyright refer to "Copyright Basics", Circular 1, US Copyright Office, Library of Congress, 101 Independence Avenure SE, Washington, DC 10559, Reviewed: 05/2012. (http://www.copyright.gov/circs/circ01.pdf, reviewed April 2013)

Remember that 'Ethical' related to doing the correct thing at the right time while 'Legal' means doing what is required by law. These terms are related, but definitely not the same.

My bottom line if you record it source it – and that precludes most concerns about plagurism and copyright. Some rules of thumb that I use are:

- If it is copied and not truly yours and it is not 'sourced' then it is plagiarized;

- If it is copied and not quoted then it is plagiarized;

- If it is 'slightly reworded' and not sourced then then it is plagiarized

Source Record

Record the source information in the selected style format. This list will become your bibliography and will be needed in the Analysis step. Make sure you record the Repository information. There are two items to record:

- The Source

- The Repository

Now you can complete what will become your foot notes or end notes so you can ethically inform the reader of the fact(s), whose fact(s) they are, what source they are in, and where they can find the source. This is especially important if you are writing the book as you research.

This record is also critical to YOUR research! In six weeks you will probably not remember where you got the information. When a new piece of information triggers an idea related to the recorded information you will want to revisit the source. With the source and repository information recorded you can easily revisit it. This will also be important if there are any questions of plagurism or copyright vioation (see the Plagurism discussion in the Information (Citation) Record and Publishing sections).

There are several recognized standard styles for recording citation, source and repository information. structuring your document in general. Major sources for this information are "The Chicago Manual of Style" and the "MLA Handbook for Writers of Research Papers, Theses, and Dissertations." Pick one that fits your writing style or that matches the requirements of your publisher. If you follow your selected standard style here you will not have to refornat the information for publishing.

Genealogical and Historical Analysis

This is where you turn your research into new knowledge! This is YOUR intelectual property and is covered by the Copyright Laws (see the discussion in the Information (Citation) Record section). New knowledge is the combination of proven information to support or disprove a hypothesis, or to answer a question. Did John Caton arrive in Virginia or Maryland?

This step is very interactive with the Genealogical Recording step. It is often easier to conduct these two steps at the same time, while the ideas and information is fresh in your mind.

If you have added sources to the previously unsupported data it is now new information. This data becomes known information and will be recorded with the source. John Caton owned land in Virginia, but there is no record when I started researching.

Record the proven assumptions, as well as the proof, as new known information. Record the disproven assumptions so you (and others) will not fall into their traps in the future! There is a Hogg Island is in New York, in Virginia in the James River near Jamestown and on the outer banks of the Maryland/Virginia Atlantic Coast! Which one did John Caton come to in 1681? There are three assumptions listed and a fourth assumption to ALWAYS consider – none of the three listed assumptions is correct!

Assumption 1 – he came to Hogg Island in the James River.

Assumption 2 – he came to Hogg Island in the Virginia County of Accomack.

Assumption 3 – he came to the Hogg Island in New York.

Unwritten Assumption 4 – he came to another Hogg Island.

We will work each of these questions through the analysis.

Source Analysis

Sources are written by people. And people have there own slant on what they observe and report. Therefore, in order to reliably use a source, we must analyze why an author wrote the information. The more reliable your sources are the more strength there is in your analysis, proof and conclusion.

There are three methods of source analysis I have used – the standard Genealogy Source Rating, the US Army Military Intelligence Rating and the rating system used in the History Department of the US Army Command and General Staff College. I tend to use all three systems to support each other. In genealogy research I focus on the Genealogy Source Rating, keeping in mind the questions raised by the other two systems.

The Genealogy Source Rating system ranks a source based on the responses to four criteria :

"Source. Choose whether the source is an original document or a transcription or translation of the original.

Clarity. Choose the legibility of the source.

Information. Choose whether this information comes from primary or secondary sources.

Evidence. Choose whether the source states a fact or requires additional evidence."

The US Army Military Intelligence Rating covers both the source and the information. Source ratings are indicated by a letter. The source portion is :

"Indicate the reliability of the source and agency as follows:

A – completely reliable.

B – usually reliable.

C – fairly reliable.

D – not usually reliable.

E – unreliable.

F – reliability cannot be judged.

A rating of "A" indicates only the most unusual circumstances For example, this evaluation is given when it is known that the source has long experience and extensive background with the type of information reported. A rating of "B" indicates a source of known integrity. A rating of

"F" indicates there is no basis for estimating the reliability of the source."

One of my favorite subject to present when I taught college courses for the US Army Command and General Staff College in Fort Leavenworth, Kansas was "Military History – Battle Analysis". Course M623-3, as it was known, includes the following :

"Having assembled the available materials, you must now evaluate your sources. This is an important step when conducting your own analysis. The author of any report or book will invariably inject some personal bias into his work. This is inevitable as the author will edit and organize his source materials prior to writing based on what he thinks is important. Although most authors strive to achieve objectivity, you must consider the author's point of view. Where does he stand on the major issues ...? Was he a participant? If not, how reliable are his sources? Was the book ... written for a particular audience? How good is the author's analysis? Did he really understand what was going on? ...

Who wrote the books and for whom?

Why and how were the books written?

What was the writer's point of view?

From whom did the writer receive advice and assistance?

Does the source provide any newly discovered evidence or a new point of view?

What are the nature and extent of the documentation of the book?

Is the book a mere reinterpretation of events based on secondary sources or an original contribution based on new or heretofore unused sources?

What areas of your assigned operation does he source cover? (Check the table of contents and index.)

How good is the analysis? Do conclusions flow logically from the evidence?"

Source Analysis Record

Record the analysis of the source using any or all of these systems. This will help you defend your conclusions. Remember that you not only have to say what you discovered, but show why you feel what you discovered is correct. This is the hidden value of recording the analysis your sources – some one will always ask 'So what makes that source so good?"!

As an example, reading the electronic copy of the original land grant to John Wharton on the Virginia Archive internet site I would provide the following source analysis:

Source – original; Clarity – clearly written; Information – primary source; Evidence – factual; Reliability – A; Credibility - ? [this is covered in the next section]; The author was responsible for maintaining a legal register of land ownership for colonial courts, the book was written at the time of registering the land grant, evidence is from claimants and surveyors, the book (and the electronic image) are original documentation completed at the time the event happened.

Remember to analyze the Repository in this record!

Information Analysis

Just because you have information does not mean it is correct. Remember those false family trees floating around the internet? And someone else may have used poor sources. Others publish invalid assumptions as facts which are often incorrect. This step precludes you from falling into these traps!

Information Analysis builds on Source Analysis. If the source is good and the information is good the fact should be good.

There is no standard genealogy information rating system I am aware of. Thus arise many great arguments on family history sites!

The US Army Military Intelligence Rating for information uses a number. When you combine the source rating and the information rating you can rank the probability that the information is valid and correct based on reliability and credibility. FM 34-3 contains a lengthy discussion on information analysis in Chapter 2 that may be useful, but is well beyond the scope of this book. Credibility ratings use the following number system:

"Indicate the credibility of information as follows:

1 – confirmed by other sources.

2 – probably true.

3 – possibly true.

4 – doubtfully true.

5 – improbable.

6 – truth cannot be judged."

Now our recorded information reads:

"John Wharton received the original land grant at the headwaters of the Blackwater River in the Colony of Maryland in Princess Anne County (not in the Black Water Plantations near Richmond) in 1680. The source is the Land Records of Colonial Maryland, Maryland Archives on the internet [refer to the full source citation recorded in the Source Record, Genealogical Recording step]. Source – original; Clarity – clearly written; Information – primary source; Evidence – factual; Reliability – A; Credibility - 2; The author was responsible for maintaining a legal register of land ownership for colonial courts, the book was written at the time of registering the land grant, evidence is from claimants and surveyors, the book (and the electronic image) are original documentation completed at the time the event happened."

Now THAT is hard to argue against!

Information Analysis Record

A basic rule I use is research is "if I do not write it down it did not happen." Just as in other disciplines I have to have the valid, reliable, creditable and verifiable information before I can state a fact. Given my memory (and most other genealogists and historians I'm sure), "I remember reading it somewhere a few months ago!" does not carry much weight in a good family page discussion or valuable family history book!

Does the information and/or analysis relate to other studies?

Now for an organization-related question – "Does this information relate to other programs or projects?" If the answer is "Yes" then Record Information and Source with other project and continue to the next step. If the answer is "No" then go to the next step.

Are the scope conditions met?

Are you ready to publish your information? If the answer is "No" then re-evaluate to see if the scope is still measurable, finite and probably attainable and restart the process. If you answer "Yes" then write up your new findings [Synthesis – What does the information mean?] and you have created historic knowledge!

<u>Publish</u>

By 'publish' I mean let others know what you have discovered! This ranges from sending an e-mail to your friends working on their genealogy search to professionally writing your family history. Information and knowledge that is not shared is lost!

A few notes here about general publication pitfalls: private information, copyright and plagiarism.

Generally private, identifying information about living individuals should NOT be published. If this type of information is incorrectly put in the public domain you may be open to legal action. For this reason, for example, Family Tree Maker provides 'privatization' processes. As another example, identifying information from censuses is not public.

Your original intellectual work – your family history information you have developed – is protected by US Federal Copyright Law. The information is protected whether your declare it by stating the information is copyrighted (like I did at the beginning of this book), registered OR NEITHER! There is a lot of information available on this subject. I recommend you research on the US Copyright Office at www.copyright.gov.

Plagiarism is an act of fraud or theft. A great source of information on plagiarism is Plagiarism.Org. They provide educational information, proper ways to use some one else's information and ways to catch plagiarists. According to Plagiarism.org (www.plagiarism.org) "According to the Merriam-Webster Online Dictionary, to "plagiarize" means

- to steal and pass off (the ideas or words of another) as one's own

- to use (another's production) without crediting the source

- to commit literary theft

- to present as new and original an idea or product derived from an existing source.

In other words, plagiarism is an act of fraud. It involves both stealing someone else's work and lying about it afterward."

CONCLUSIONS

Genealogy and History Project Definition and Process

This book is focused on the amateur genealogist and historian. Because of that, I have not delved into the depths of Project Management related to the total discipline of Genealogy or History. For major genealogical programs and projects, as well as profession genealogists and historians, I strongly recommend further study of project management and certification as a Project Management Professional with the Project Management Institute.

Using the PMI definitions and processes of Project Management in the Genealogy and History Disciplines, the definition of a Genealogy and History Project becomes the study and publication of the results of research of the history of an individual, specific family group (as defined by a specific number of generations), or geographic area with specific geographic boundaries and timeframe. By overlaying a simplified Project Management Process over the Genealogy and History Research Process, we get the Anderson Genealogy Process.

The Anderson Genealogy Process uses the previously defined genealogy processes as tools to reach and publish supportable conclusions and observations about family history. We now have a way to structure and manage our research that is measurable, manageable and rigorous.

Not only that – it is simple, easy, and fits into the use of the other genealogy and history tools as well the documents available. Who knows – you may publish the next definitive scholarly history of your family!

How Can I Use a Genealogy Program?

I am not referring to a computer application. In Genealogy, History and Project Management we can start with a big question or program and break it down to projects. We can also group related projects, using what has been developed as a Genealogy or History Project, to develop a larger Genealogical Program! We can study all of the generations on a family line by dividing the line into groups of generations. Or we can study all the family members in a geographic area, then put them together in a Genealogical Program to write a book later. However you would like to group your projects that make sense! Each project could make a great chapter in the program to produce the definitive family history book!

Why do these concepts strengthen each other?

By using Project Management with a fully defined disciplinary (Genealogy and/or History) process, we can now professionally identify a desired result and manage the cost, time and scope to successfully reach and support the conclusion. We can reliably project what the outcome will be, when it will be, and what it should cost.

We have broken out of the "never-ending genealogy process" and now have a definable set of processes that give us a reusable method to produce a result. We can now say "Let's write a family book. Dan, you take the Caton Families in Mound City, MO. Margie, you take the FitsRandolph Families directly related to the Caton Family. We have $500 to spend and the book will be self-published in 6 months." We now have one Genealogy and History Program (the family book) of two Genealogy Projects. And I'm sure there will be many subprojects developed to publish our Best Seller!

And now?

I hope this provides you with a new set of useful tools to may your study of family history both enjoyable, and productive. HAPPY 'GENEATING'!

BIBLIOGRAPHY AND END NOTES

Bibliography

About Genealogy, http://genealogy.about.com.

"ANCESTORS – The Research Process", A Production of BYU Broadcasting, 2005, Brigham Young University, 2005, ISBN 1-59156-831-5.

"Copyright Basics", Circular 1, US Copyright Office, Library of Congress, 101 Independence Avenure SE, Washington, DC 10559, Reviewed: 05/2012

Dictionary.com. Dictionary.com Unabridged (v 1.1). Random House, Inc. http://dictionary.reference.com.

"Field Manual (FM) 34-3 Intelligence Analysis", Department of the Army, Washington, DC, 15 March 1990, Approved for public release; distribution is unlimited.

"Guide to the Project Management Body of Knowledge (PMBOK Guide), A", Third Edition, 2004, Project Management Institute, Newton Square, PA 19073; ISBN 193069950-6.

"In Search of Family History: A Starting Place" by Paul Drake, J. D.; 2nd Ed., Heritage Books, Inc., Bowie, Maryland; 1992; ISBN 1-55613-718-4; Midwest Historical and Genealogical Society, Wichita, KS Call No. I-54.

"M623-3 Military History – Battle Analysis"; Combat Studies Institute, U.S. Army command and General Staff College; Fort Leavenworth, KS; 20 March, 1996.

"Official Guide to Family Tree Maker 2008, The", Lord, Tana Pedersen; Ancestry Publishing, Provo, UT; 2007, ISBN- 10: 1-59331-310-1.

Plagiarism.org, web site www.plagiarism.org

"Practical Research: Planning and Design"; Leedy, Paul D,; Fifth Edition; Prentice-Hall, Inc., Upper Saddle River, NJ, USA; 1993; ISBN: 0-02-369242-1

Wikipedia, http://en.wikipedia.org.

End Notes

I - -logy. Dictionary.com. Dictionary.com Unabridged (v 1.1). Random House, Inc. http://dictionary.reference.com/b-rowse/-logy (accessed: February 13, 2008).

ii - http://en.wikipedia.org/wiki/Genealogy, 15 February, 2008.

Iii - "A Guide to the Project Management Body of Knowledge (PMBOK Guide)", Third Edition, 2004, Project Management Institute, Newton Square, PA 19073; ISBN 193069950-6; page 20.

iv - Ibid.

v - PMBOK, page 26.

vi - Leedy, Paul D,; "Practical Research: Planning and Design"; Fifth Edition; Printice-Hall, Inc., Upper Saddle River, NJ, USA; 1993; ISBN: 0-02-369242-1

vii - Leedy, Paul; Practical Research: Planning and Design, page 12.

viii - Ibid, pages 16-18.

ix - Ibid, pages 16-17 and Figure 1.1 page 17.

x - Ibid, page 16 and Figure 1.2 page 18.

xi - "ANCESTORS – The Research Process", A Production of BYU Broadcasting, 2005, Brigham Young University, 2005, ISBN 1-59156-831-5.

xii - http://genealogy.about.com/cs/research/a/process.htm, 16 February 2008

xiii - PMBOK, page 383.

xiv - PMBOK, page 383.

xv - PMBOK, page 392.

xvi - Leedy, page 332.

xvii - Leedy, page 332.

xviii - "The Official Guide to Family Tree Maker 2008", page 98.

xix - "FM 34-4 Intelligence Analysis", page 2-15.

xx - "M623-3", pages Adv 3-1-1 and Adv 3-1-2.

Xxi - "FM 34-4 Intelligence Analysis", page 2-15.

Xxii - www.plagiarism.org, as of 24 March, 2008.

NOTES

ABOUT THE AUTHOR

Daniel G. Anderson is a certified Project Management Professional (PMP) by the Project Management Institute (PMI) and received a MA in Computer Systems and Information Systems Management for Webster University.

Dan is a retired US Army officer who settled with his wife in Wichita, Kansas and they are active in the history community of the area. When he taught the US Army Reserve Command and General Staff College courses for eight years he lead discussions about analyzing and writing military history papers. He is the Vice President for Programs for the Midwest Historical and Genealogical Society in Wichita. As the facilitator he has lead a discussion group that shares information on genealogy and family history writing. His is also a Freemason and the Executive Director of the Midwest Historic Masonic Lodge Association, Inc.

As an amateur genealogist and historian, he has brought together three disciplines and shared the results in a set of useful tools for those who identify, record, analyze and publish genealogical and historical information.